# THE TENDERNESS
# AND THE WOOD

GUERNICA WORLD EDITIONS 28

The author gratefully acknowledges grants from the
National Endowment for the Arts and the ConaCulta
(Mexico's National Endowment) for *The Tenderness and the Wood*

# THE TENDERNESS AND THE WOOD

Marlon L. Fick

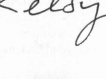

For my young, beautiful
and smart friend
Kelsy

2020

**GUERNICA**
**World**
**EDITIONS**

TORONTO—CHICAGO—BUFFALO—LANCASTER (U.K.)
2020

Michael Mirolla, editor
Cover design: Allen Jomoc Jr.
Interior layout: Jill Ronsley, suneditwrite.com
Cover Concept: Marlon L. Fick
Cover Art: *Woman and Swallow*, Francisca Esteve
Guernica Editions Inc.
287 Templemead Drive, Hamilton (ON), Canada L8W 2W4
2250 Military Road, Tonawanda, N.Y. 14150-6000 U.S.A.
www.guernicaeditions.com

Distributors:
Independent Publishers Group (IPG)
600 North Pulaski Road, Chicago IL 60624
University of Toronto Press Distribution,
5201 Dufferin Street, Toronto (ON), Canada M3H 5T8
Gazelle Book Services, White Cross Mills
High Town, Lancaster LA1 4XS U.K.

First edition.
Printed in Canada.

Legal Deposit—Third Quarter
Library of Congress Catalog Card Number: 2019949706
Library and Archives Canada Cataloguing in Publication
Title: The tenderness and the wood / Marlon L. Fick.
Names: Fick, Marlon L., 1960- author.
Description: Series statement: Guernica world editions ; 28
Identifiers: Canadiana 20190181680 | ISBN 9781771835565 (softcover)
Subjects: LCGFT: Poetry.
Classification: LCC PS3606.I25 T46 2020 | DDC 811/.6—dc23

*for Robert Bly*

# Contents

# About The Tenderness and the Wood

MARLON L. FICK rejected religion at a very young age despite having what he believed were mystical experiences, only to return to what he considered a middle ground: Jamesian pluralism and Christian agnosticism. Also, from a very young age, he was consumed by Walt Whitman, Rilke, and San Juan de la Cruz—poets who were to become his personal predecessors. But the directions these poets take is, in Fick's work, quite the opposite: Fick says that all of the world's religions began as lyric poetry, which was then later bastardized when codified for the sake of collective narratives. He realized this upon discovering Blake's *The Marriage of Heaven and Hell*. Fick works backwards through religion's perversions and discarded shells to its original purity—in the process, his poetry echoes T.S. Eliot's description of Baudelaire's "high blasphemy." "I Am Fly," "The Tenderness and the Wood," and other poems demonstrate it clearly: A very small fly, with a massive vocabulary, buzzes about a cathedral proclaiming that he, alone, is his "ownmost teleos." It's not the only time Fick dwells ironically on themes of self-deception and loss, but with an unmatched sleight of hand for sustained, intellectual metaphors. Ultimately, Fick's quest resembles Rilke more than Eliot, the latter he used to imitate in his youth; Rilke's "terrifying angels" here appear as "swallows." They appear, disappear, and are followed but never found. The pilgrimage is a walk down city streets, down vast expanses of time, but there can never be a destination or "a still point."

The "tenderness" and "wood" signify both sex and crucifixion without redemption, passion without any purpose other than itself, the harsh reality of "love" and "sex." At the age of sixteen, the books of Sartre and Camus made a lasting imprint of Fick's worldview, one, which Fick explains, is a view from which he has never recovered.

The poems in *The Tenderness and the Wood* received the National Endowment in 2005; earlier versions of the same poems received Mexico's National Endowment in 2000, the ConaCulta; since then the manuscript was chosen seven times as a finalist for the Dorset Prize, along with the publisher's promise to nominate the work for The National Book Prize. His loyalty to Tupelo ended up delaying its publication for many years until his friend, Greg Geis, convinced him to send the work to Guernica, in Canada. In fact, some of the poems have been written and re-written since the middle 1970s. In 1984, his teacher at NYU, the literary critic M. L. Rosenthal, wrote "Fick has sustained the visionary moment longer than any poet since Ezra Pound's 'Rock Drill Cantos.'" Poets and critics since then—among them, Jonathan Holden and Dana Gioia—have made similar claims, stating that Fick deserves a place alongside the major poets. Still, he goes largely unknown in his own country. Here, in Mexico, he is respected and honored. In 1997, after receiving a letter from Robert Hass about Fick, Octavio Paz invited Fick to read at Palacio de Bellas Artes. The press covered his progress here widely, and he published his first three books in Mexico.

Willis Barnstone wrote an introduction to the first version of *Tenderness*, but it was never used:

> Marlon Fick is not a poet of one day. He is a poet of centuries, voices, scriptures, and revelations. After the tragic loss of his wife and daughter, he became a single being beset by being, alone, without a witnessing deity, with others and without them, with poets and with himself. He is an American from the University of Kansas (and NYU) on his world vagabondage as Hemingway came from the university of the Midwest and its telegraph office, and went on to mix with continents. Both Fick and Hemingway are clearly from the university of the world; and just as the hunter/writer Hemingway is likely to mix John Donne's and Marvell's phrases (*The Sun Also Rises, For Whom the Bell Tolls*) into his own atlas and telegraphic style, so too,

in the Gospel of Marlon, the authors of the world help the wanderer survive and prosper in art. His long cantos speed with verve and astonishment, with poems inside of poems, and in turn, yet other poems in poems, like the "multifoliate rose" of T.S. Eliot. Or like Arthur Rimbaud he invents his mad lucidity as he wakes to dreams of the unlikely and beautiful and terrible, and as in Robert Desnos, the surrealist poet always in realistic love, he compels with a passion that never diminishes. Fick is likely to show up in a village in the Congo and just as likely to pop up in a Mexican market place next to a Zapotec on her knees, or at midnight walking the Calle de Francisco de Madero to the Zocalo of Aztec and La Nueva España Mexico, or now with young women in a Pakistani university, who will listen and learn by his words the inevitable passion for life expressed when content mystically reaches out and touches form. Wherever he is, he creates his gospel, his good news, which is an original one. I urge you to read him, hear him, remember the words, and linger in the epiphanies.

Clearly, Barnstone perceived the sweeping expanse of the poems, and the man himself as a journeyman, a modern Provençal. Soon after Pakistan, Fick traveled back to Latin America, and then to China, then to Spain and France—always conscious that, like Stevens, his poems might seem to be more about places than people, and that Sartre's "hell as 'other'" chases him no matter where he is. I happen to know he keeps in his wallet a scrap of paper with a poem by Rukkert, "An die Musik," that was set to music by Shubert. The two of us were sitting under a fig tree one autumn day in Cuernavaca when he took it out and read it. When he finished, he said, "That's all there is, you know." He never privileges one poet over another, which is why he devoted every weekend for a year to me at a borrowed house south of Mexico City, for the sole purpose of translating my first book into English and getting me accepted at Sarah Lawrence, meanwhile introducing me to Ellen Bryant Voigt and Tom Lux. As Barnstone indicated, he is—like Pound—a tireless champion of other poets. After two years in China, he returned to the United States, having translated China's premier poet, Ouyang Jianghe, which he followed with an edition and translation of 14 Catalan poets, *XEIXA* (Tupelo Press, 2018).

Fick IS the terrifying angel, the swallow, the crow "gnashing his beak" against the primordial stone to make the first spark. Ironically, his life chased after his poetry, catching up with him on a Friday afternoon in Lahore, Pakistan. The Taliban set off a bomb by his car. We think he was their target, but the bomb took the lives of twenty-five school children, his body guard, his colleague, his chauffeur. He walked away with minor physical injuries, hearing loss, and major memory loss. After suffering a near total loss of his own identity, he wrote himself back into existence. Only words could save him. After spending a few days with Robert Bly, in intimate conversations, like "two men, speaking low in a boat," Fick continued on his journey. I wasn't present for those conversations, but he relayed, in passing, "Bly said not to try to make sense out of things that don't make sense." It was all he needed to hear and perhaps it is all his reader needs to know, for now.

*Francisco Avila*

# I Am Fly

I am Fly
and there is no God.
I am Fly, the smart, dark angel with transparent wings,
green and purple eyes.
I need no one.

Still I confess
I'm drawn to the calling of a violin, the fragile
       shoulders, the tight wire of a female voice.
I swoop through the air to find it, enter it, probe it,
gorge
       and purge.
I am fly, so
naturally I'm curious.

I alone am why, my ownmost teleos.
Draw my own circles,
lived in Miro's brain,
annoyed Wittgenstein with the now-you-see-me-now-you-don't
       uncertainties,
went for a swim in the tea in T.S. Eliot's cup.

Now this doll thinks that I don't know she's there;
the she doll in her doll house waiting rooms, waits,
her eternal torment, expectation,
       and gazes blankly to the end of the earth's last spasm.
Desolation and de-
composition.

Oh I am in love. I am Fly—
          vertiginous, sumptuous, prodigious!
I never blink
and have no memories.
I interrogate at random.
Born on a dead star, abandoned nest
of obscurity and contamination, dreamed
          into existence by the very thing I seek, the void, woman,
crossing and uncrossing her legs. There
is my altar, there
the silk trampoline
          my vault and somersault
                    my dart and thrust
                              the anonymous bed ...

There I alight and play with her hair, the strings of music
in sugary blue light
snaking through the air
          like frankincense, glass
bodies of illuminated saints, in pieces, watching,
but who can't see with their glass eyes
the vague bed
          woven just for me, the white or black of a woman's skin
and many arms
of memories, poor motherless cross,
          bright compass of snow.

I am Fly. I fly and nurse,
lips black and pursed—eyes more languorous auras of the blood
     tumescent
with the images of crimes—eyes panoramic
technicolored eyes that see beyond the halo of horizons to
     apocalypse.

I have carried the plague in my hands to the sleepless.
Now let me be entwined in her bandages,
        wound round in silk
                and spun into another world.
Let me dissolve in her blood, her waiting rooms, her bog
        of paradise.
Infinitesimal speck of excrement, I sign my name
        and who can say that I was ever here?
Who?
        To allow me the last supper
which anyway I can't eat and would spit out
like a bitter moon upon my sticky tongue,
a small, flat world of desert languages
and the stale, moldy bodies that spoke them.

Was a time the world buzzed with it, laughing at a joke
        inside a womb,
but the promised land is a desert now, or
cathedral where, I gather,
        some savior lies, guarded like a lock
of baby hair.

The first shall be last, saith Fly.
Whatever that means.

# One Never Knows

One never knows ...
I pass a church made from sheets of metal
and no windows, stained or otherwise ...

Maybe it wasn't a church after all
but a strip club.
They look pretty much the same.

And what goes on in there?
I suppose there is music, all sorts of praise, donations, and
a lot of halleluiahs and speaking in tongues with the eyes rolled
    back in ecstasy.

Whatever it is, we want to peel away the layers
to get at something more.
We want it bare on a bear skin rug
or hanging from a pole or crucifix we can fix our gaze upon
    in quiet, respectful, irreverence.

# The Tenderness and the Wood

They were not the same dreams, yours and mine.
In yours I am homeless and just looking for a bed.
In mine it's simpler.
I'm a lover, a solicitous pet.
The windows are open, shutters winking furtively.
I enter and find you naked, old, but in excellent good health.
And the sweat is sexual.
We have washed up on an island.
We are the mended egg. Two fish as a circle
in the abyss
before geometry, turning its back and shoulders to the sun.

My last thoughts in this life were of you—
an eclipse of sun-eating cats
littering the embalmer's work room floor
with the last minute notes of afterthoughts,
the opaque remnants of a pair of eyes staring out in amazement …
how far away … the curious attraction to the universe, the giant
    wound
we walk to on the wooden legs of telescopes.

Then everyone who passed, passed muttering,
and I could hear songs hermetically sealed in dusty wells,
and so I cast a spell that would weaken you almost to the point of
    death
so you would call for me, but now
the setting was a "hill faraway"
and I came in as a cat, squeezing through the window
where your bed is warm from fever.

In both dreams we are lost.
In both our father is a crow
gnashing his beak to make sparks.
And he took us to see the auroras
because before we did not know colors.
We knew only the before before before.
We did not know we were two.
We did not know *male* from *female*
or *flower* from *animal*.
We were the stars where they were aligned.
Hill of thunder and incandescence.
Hill we rolled down in play to be drunk with vertigo
        in the bluestem, buffalo, and tickle grass—
making circles in the wind.
Hill with the cross of a man and a woman without shame,
the woman pinned to the man, the axis resplendent,
        motionless, quiet—
who knelt, kissed, and made a sacrifice of scattered nails.

# The Swallows of Barcelona

Forgive me,
I didn't mean to walk so far I couldn't come home
but when you have lived long enough, among others,
no one notices or talks to an old man.
Morning reaches the church windows, stained with lies.
Tired saints and honest swallows, a girl who lay with strangers all
    night
walks home, bitter between the legs.

We try to hold on like ivy climbing the wall of a gray façade
and iron bars of balconies,
but when you have lived enough among others,
with winter and solitude, or a woman you loved so long
it becomes an old song,
you have lived until all you have left are wings that hurt.

Somewhere it's raining carnations.
Couples amble on the avenues, wearing Ferris wheels.
They have not heard the news:
Swallows full of grace, born from the blue, bearing our sorrow
    serenely.

# Winter Signs

Some mornings when I roused him
he could stand bold upright, still sleeping
as I wrapped him in his clothes, his head
poking through the portals of T-shirt and sweater
into the conscious world, chin up, eyes closed.
Then I kissed him on the nose and said "good morning."
He'd looked up at me, wondering perhaps
if I were his real father, which
he would wonder again in his teens.

We'd go out with the dog in the overcast
past a row of houses with identical gray roofs
and windows frosted over like the clouded eyes of dying fish.
Dead leaves skipped in the street behind us.
Other leaves were wet and frozen.
His mother lived like that for many years, quiet, overcast.

And then it snowed
and everything lost its focus.
It snowed to even a score or to blind us
to the dark that lives inside.

I taught him how to read the signs:
an empty nest,
a set of tracks bounding away.
Skin-sack and bones of a mouse chucked back by an owl.
Vole shit in the crossroads of small tunnels
they burrowed through the snow to escape.

Once there was a bed,
some leaves and patches of shed fur
where two deer had lain the night before on needles.
They do not mate in winter, not even to stay warm.
My son looked at the impression they made,
clutching his stuffed rabbit by the neck.
I looked at him looking at the empty bed, his pink nose running
with sap. The animal, real or not real, boy or man …
Maybe it's this way with hawks that stand and watch,
hungry to feel the warm fur close; it doesn't matter whose.

# The Flood

The cattle are locked in their bodies
when the water comes.
They get their hooves stuck in the mud and sink.
The titanic bodies swell,
and their swollen tongues are like the river itself,
too muddy to reflect the setting sun,
too cloudy to reflect on anything.

The fields are underwater.
The water comes to change us.
Thistles to anemones, and the sunflowers
with their underwater love-me-nots,
it leaves it that way, between loves.

Don't come near me.
This is not about desire.
I was thinking about the human voices
and the wheat under water still golden
because it doesn't know it's drowned yet,
and the alfalfa fields, and the Milo fields.

I found a snake hole one summer and poured water down it
and waited ...
and nothing happened ...
the flood, or otherwise the year of nothing, leaving nothing in its
   wake.

Up here in the Sierra Mountains
a man waters all day a tree that died a year ago.

Maybe the flood came for the same reason, to be
the so-it-goes.

As when the river keeping its peace,
flowing between monotonous banks, suddenly says,
"No, this is not all I need!"

Not the way God reaches tenderly toward Adam,
but clinched, ready to possess,
to strip the land of its sex,
to reach beyond to what belongs to each of them
(books, photographs, the child they bore together)
and divide.

In cycles we came around,
turning in the casual void to the answers—
two of us, not one,
shuddering a little when the darkness reaches,
its fingers dividing like torn trees
when they drag the water for what is lost.

# Waking Up in Djidji

Morning.
I'm standing in the door of my house,
waking slowly in a house made of mud and wattles.

In Africa,
the flame trees are too bright to see.

Day breaks like a fever.
Birds cover themselves in the canopy and call.

Last night drummed such celebration
that now I'm sad,
unable to explain …

A gazelle hangs from a post in a cloud of black flies, suspended …

A small child pounds open palm nuts with a stone
for her grandmother to make into wine.
She doesn't look up from her work.

Her sister still sleeps in my bed.
Juliette, fifteen.
Mbulu's third wife and pregnant with his child,
or mine.

I remember a letter Paul Gauguin
wrote to Van Gogh in which he says he has
"a taste for the primitive."

Perhaps I will write a letter today.

Or maybe I will go down to the river to wash the sweet night
    off my skin.

# Puget Sound

We reach for the smallest things first:
a wing bone from a sea gull, pieces
of kelp that break apart easily.
We hardly notice the afternoon
spreading itself too thinly across the Sound,
making the bright bones dark,
like the dark bones in each finger
of each hand.

I've been up late
listening to the steady notes of a ferry
sound and release. It holds on
for a moment and releases, like
your love for me.
I'm standing on the shore, wanting
to see between notes.
You never made me restless.
Perhaps the waves, close and away, remain.

Perhaps, I'm learning that the shore
is never right
and so is always shifting.
And promises are all washed up.

# Somewhere to Sit in Mexico City

Lord give me somewhere to sit in Mexico City,
give me a little café
away from the cars
where the loose odors of coffee and perfume
darken and bloom in the air.

Let Michael the shoeshine man
establish his throne
on the corner
and have me ascend with the daily news.

And let Fernanda the prostitute
stop and talk for a while, with her eyes
that reflect the October rain.

The years have worn against her, too.

Bring me an old book
          and a little tobacco,

and let a fichus leaf fall in my lap.

# Melissa's White Dress

When I was a child
I dozed off to sleep in the snow.
I was warm and began to drift like the snow itself.

Now, years later, I'm late to rise in the morning
and a little thin with grief.
Mornings in the mirror a coyote looks back at me
from a field of stubble—

he stalks the faint gray shadow of a mouse
and lopes out of the field to the woods
where the snow is always last to leave,
blue in the valley where it lingers.

Then I phone Melissa, who is a lot younger than I am
and never home
or never existed, married in my mind with winter,
my longing to drift.

# The Angel over Mexico City

All night cars cross both ways
on the Avenue of Reforma
making the fanatical sign of the cross—
then park, alarms trumpeting …
We get out of our beds.
The dawn is as gray as a body in the morgue
and the wings on the Angel of Reforma stay still.
Nothing moves her.

The sun rises,
rolling back white like an eye born blind at birth.
I wake out of a sleep
which was a tomb robbed of its dreams,
a night with its statuesque angels, panderers, and prostitutes;
night with its eye, a dying star.

Mornings I pass a child
in the tunnel of *Insurgentes*
and buy white roses that are turning brown.
This morning she carried a doll upside down by a plastic foot
like a nurse with a stillborn baby. Its white nylon
parachutes upside down. It hasn't a gender.
One of the angels that didn't make it.

I think the blue eyes of its world are closed
or have swiveled back around to examine
where the brain would be.

\* \* \*

Likewise

four men from Papantla
tether their feet to a pole
and swing upside down to the music
of wooden flutes and small drums silly with joy.

There was a summer so hot that only the flies
had motion. I caught them out of boredom,
tied them to threads
and let them buzz around in circles.

The song can make you dizzy.

One day in a train leaving Seville Station
I saw Margarito, no bigger than
a three month old, in his late sixties.
He came up to my knees.
I'd heard of him but thought he wasn't real—just apocryphal
like the Virgin of Guadalupe.
He made his way down the aisle with a toy guitar,
strumming on plastic strings and singing like a sparrow.

It was a small cruelty,
but so was the song.

*    *    *

One day, for example, riding the escalator
in *Barranca del Muerto* I felt
its steel teeth chewing backwards through time.

I remembered the accordions of locusts
I heard them in the half-ratchets
of the twisted tridents of the turnstiles
like clocks wound back violently.

What was it I remembered?
The accordion child,
the child who holds out his hand for a peso,
the woman beading her sweat
and weaving her veins.
Millions were climbing out of their valleys,
secretaries, accountants … raising their heads toward the
    florescent light
not like saints but tired people
coming from the office—

So there was light, I told them.
Nothing was lost. Only the walls
grew thin like the pine of an old guitar.
The apartment walls took on random constellations:
the *ts* of my typewriter traveling up to apartments above
and coming back to me love cries, shouting,
children horsing around, crashing of dishes,
the colicky infant, a boy beating time
with his head—against the wall.

One night
Señora Araceli appeared at my door
with a bag of curtains
so that we might see and hear less.
I didn't know if they were meant
for the one looking in or looking out.

Then this morning I was telling my students
they must say the conjugations of *have* and *be*
as if they were saying the rosary.
A chorus scales the walls—sirens
trace the valleys, graphing the jags of the heart,
the staccato yips of a poodle,
the hurry of rats, their little white hands

thrumming their thumbs like a flicker of candles in a church.
Sounds that are given to me
as if they were mine *to have* and *to be.*

*   *   *

The village gathered to look in the mirror of the camera.
In the middle they have positioned a wooden box.
Inside the box, an infant.
The camera blinks
and returns to darkness.

The eye reverses what it sees: sees

Not easy to hear this.
Sound travels away
like those men swung around by a foot,
like a doll with a plastic song or a very small man.

It travels the speed of light so it bends.
It points in the other direction like the thorns of bougainvillea.

Invisible.

The eyes in the street open wider till they do not notice.

# Anniversary

This evening an indolent wind moves between us
where you hanged yourself
in the stars like chimes.

There is an empty plot my eyes console
where witch-grass cripples with frost
and mums mingle with the moonlight lavender.

With what celerity the mathematicians
count as lost, snow undertakes your silence.
Now another woman kisses me.
Her lips
are the rim of your grave.
My nights are destruction and wind
Moaning across an empty bell.

I found you everywhere, the hunt
as winter, the one the world prays to
or will undress for, the snow
our bodies melt
into
flower-water.

# The Sources of Light

Mornings before dawn I rose
and lit the kerosene lantern
and took the pole from a corner in the barn
and then went down a road through the fields to a creek where
it bent around behind a hedge of Osage Orange.

After setting the line
I built a fire to keep mosquitoes away,
and fished for an hour or two, often for nothing.

I was ten and confident and I thought
all sources of light had a common ancestor in God:
my lantern;
the lights in the town in the valley,
flashes from firecrackers inches away from my fingers;
the searing of lightning
               crossing the plains on crooked legs ...

I thought these held in common some
memory of the stars
before they were broken into a million pieces—

like the fireflies I gathered in a jar
to read by phosphorus ...
that same light belonging to corn
whose fuses flared more gold against black clouds,
and more green before they died.

I didn't know how wrong I was
or when I knew each light
in the valley
had a life circling around it like a small, gray moth.

I walked straight into the light that only the dying see,
that covers itself up in forever
and burns in all the others.

# A Priori to His Will

*for Greg Geis*

He left me his guitars
and hearing aids
so my fingers could fret over loss
and my ears remember his laugh.
So I listened and strummed in limbo
to his thoughts, the table talk, Pascal
       and Martin Luther going out on a thin limb,
when, really, he and I were on the thinnest limb of all,
bearing the weight of the past,
summers of love
and summers of no love.
And winters when a rose would bloom.

And when I listened to my friend,
God came in the room—that is, He, his searing fountain, jetsam of
    image and idea.

And I learned—listening through his ears—of transformation:
The portal of light inside blindness that drives the swift,
    benevolent star past time itself.

# Crows

Crows love midwinter mornings
as do I
staggering, black
and shiny—out of their asylum.
Mornings so cold the air is seized
in the impasse
of its bitterness, a white, violet mist.

They drop from the naked trees for what remains.
Suet that hangs in a cage,
tethered to a limb.
Too bright, like lacquered boxes.
Too bright the shine on them.
Not yet defined from darkness.

We hope for what we understand,
pain that comes and goes and comes like winter,
in welcomed revelations.
A cardinal blooming on a January thorn.
Doves weeping, eating seeds that rained through cracks.
Sparrows purchased for pennies in Jerusalem
and eaten by the poor. It's what we
learned by repetition, first having, then
not having. Seeing
and not seeing.
Not a force of darkness spinning on beyond our reach.

Jesus says to live like crows.
I'm remembering the sermon

as one of them jabs its black beak in the suet.
Don't worry a minute of your life.
Don't gather stores for winter.
. Don't plant or harvest.
But the other birds are worried. A blue jay swoops
under a nearby pine, shrill with jealousy. And
a sparrow in a leafless redbud is occupied by a mute terror.

In another account by the French explorer, de Crèvecoeur,
crows leave a man with his eyes picked out,
staring out of nothing at the empty horizon.

I'm outside.
I'm shivering.
I begin not to understand the need I have
to gather details.
That rabbis, for example, forbid mentioning crows in prayer.
Or Pliny thinking crows were absent minded
and couldn't find their way back home.

It's staggering.
I can't stop shivering.

# Zócalo As the Sun Goes Down

Shadows slant like pyramids
shorn in two where we have met
at dusk
to walk the labyrinth, the Zócalo.
                             Splintered bones
of light
cast down in prophesy. Cocoons suspended
in the copal smoke
are washed away in the next millennium.
Supplications of the cup and flame.

I confess I don't know
what any of this means to you,
       the streets in nervous crisis,
       whores with a look that says nothing.

The petals of the amber sun may never
open up to us,
       nor the embryo etherized in stone
       awaken in the *joyerías* where the gold surrounds us
in the anterooms of afterlife.

Stone fragments
            slumped back
to the undulations of their given shapes.

We cross Madero, where the news
on dirty shrouds
is clothes pinned to the corner stands.

It hardly matters what it says:
a university still closed, more police,
another Beatle nearly murdered.
It's not that different from a Latin mass:
either way the meanings are assumed.
Even our prayers can be reduced to numbers
and assigned to days.
There are no symbols anymore. A thousand windows
and not one
remembers its dreams.

All the promises of the sun
        flicker in the chimes'
shed wings.
        Children living down a hole in acrid pools
like a lost codex for what might have been—
how near their end is to beginning.
But they light the world with silverfish,
paint the sun in black
and live.

I want to look at them for once, without looking away.
For once … follow a scar that shines in the east.
The circles in their eyes like tree rings petrified by silence
in the margins of another world—
an animal, half-man, unearthed from sleep,
tiny manhole of his eye rolled back

                    but windows weren't invented yet

                        *   *   *


and no one saw
and no wind had a name

only grass
and a cool blue darkness like a snake …

*   *   *

The salvages are all we know,
the broken jars,
a heart dried into dust.

To the Greeks, meaning formed
in the union of two halves.

To say this
we are torn. We are this sunset.
The passing red and yellow rags.
The martyr in his death-by-fire forever kingdom.
Neither here nor there.

Nor there.
A woman in patches of blue.
A man or a woman buried alive in dark, voluminous mirrors.

It's your city
and so your meaning, formed in the vague wake,
crowning pawnshops
and houses of the poor, the *tiendas* shivering
with love songs.

Walk with me and be my eyes
and tell me again
how everything we love turns colors right before it dies.

# Postcards from Winter

I left a watchman at Place de St. Michel
to guard the beautiful boy I was,
the one with long blond hair
who played and sang his heart out to a crowd.

Along the way I wrote postcards to myself.
On one,
"There is a crow between us."

On another,
"poppies
blooming in a field of wheat."

Sometimes,
just a lovely word, or two,
*lilac* and *wisteria.*
More words could ruin everything.

They all came back, one by one
like people queuing up to nod beside a burial
for someone we hardly knew.

*Would you mind, terribly, if I wear my wedding ring?*
*I mean my former one?*
*Not yours, I mean, the one that has a diamond?*

Why not?

It has the brilliance of a star, and both the diamond and the star
are light years from the boy I used to be.

*What are you writing?! What?!*

A rat in Châtelet is more beautiful than my life.

# Lent

I shall be the ashes on your forehead,
I shall be your sacrifice for Lent, your suffering,
your joy, the intimate thing you betrayed in telling God.

If we are truly one
       from the same, hollow egg,
the original violation
the something from nothing
if we were
       to have turned from one to two,
when one meets two
       some midnight rendezvous
then I'd go on in ordinary time.

But please understand, down here
everything is upside down—
the pansies bloom in February
       or they were put there by an unseen hand.
(I have named them all after you.)

Here is where all the angels and saints go to winter,
where I have only to write about the weather
where there is no weather
but the burnt hours of *ofrendas*.

       Although, surrounded by signs,
I have learned it is better to have no faith:
it's the pigeon's fate

to hop from its nest off a tenth story ledge.
I prefer the certain death of life here on the ground,
the cradle of broken glass.
                              Those green
necklaces of beads on blossoms of jacaranda will,
by Pascua,
turn to worms and crawl from their graves to the light
to feast on the leaves until there is nothing left
but gnawed bones,
transferences,
copies,
copies of copies without origin.
You asked me once if I'd ever been in love.
You asked me more than once.
Is it spring or still winter where you are?
I've lost my calendar.
A thief stole my watch in the subway.
By nights I wander the city alone.
The lampposts glare at me.
By day I wander the same streets, stopping to rest
in the gardens where you are not and have never been,
and I carry a book
        that has not been written, that a dog
has chewed
out of hunger and curiosity.
And I sit on a bench made for two and think
*the bench is made for two ...*
The answer is not in my book.
I have tunneled through to the margins and fallen off.

Is it time? Is this the time beyond margins?
Are your seasons something like a codex of being,
the four quadrants? or the two, the *not yet* and *no longer*?

Up there right side up, do the families
and their pagan offspring
          go on picnics, and do they gorge
and the little ones grow sick on colored eggs?

You think I am the unholy vice,
          the dark, equatorial compass, the tilt of the earth …
and because I cannot form beyond shadows …
I shall surely disappear in the light of reason.
They say in the white, wooden churches, we receive
a thousand thousand times
that which we have given out in charity.
So I will stay, and cleave,
and be the ashes on your forehead.

# Temptation

Mothers of Jerusalem,
look after your children.

*In my father's house there are many rooms ...*

This time of year the moon can draw the blood of unclean men
through stone resolve ...

*I go to prepare a bed for you ...*

Three surrendered to the sea and like magic disappeared.

*And if I go to prepare a bed for you*
*I will come again*
*and take you, and bring you close to me.*

Perhaps you are not real
but neither am I
and my imagination has betrayed us both.

\*　\*　\*

Wednesday, I wrote the original shibboleth in the sand
and watched it dissolve and felt loss—
the name my father gave me.

And then went back to remain unnamed
and wait for Thursday,
reading late

the gentleman's magazines where all is revealed—
　　　　pressed flowers,
icons of desire, the deserts of heaven, posed ecstasy,
pages illuminated and worn
under the bed where I sleep and float on that long ago dead sea.

# Parting Words

*Do they know what they do?*

You tell me not to send you gifts
after you have given me so much.

I bought a small black cross of *acerina.*

You tell me not to write for forty days.
I'm your sacrifice for *forty days of doom and gloom.*

After forty days I rise and telephone.
You tell me not to call
so I don't call
and you call me and ask me to come.

I bought a humble bowl for alms and left it
carefully wrapped
in foreign language newspapers
and the postman, thinking it was for him, never came back.

Now you dance when you sing
and tell me I should not have come home
to the land that was my father's land.
You imagine I still love you
after you set fire to the land and burned my letters.
I suppose I do.

But I was only made of words, not places.
You turned me to smoke
and my spirit had nowhere to go.
            Like you
a Kansas wind,
the coyote you hear in the distance
            who tells you something is missing ...
You, Gypsy! It was your freedom I loved.
That you crossed a desert in Africa.

*I am thirsty.*

The same year I hid in the Congo in a small, mud house, and read
the letters you never wrote back.

*Why have you forsaken me?*

This black cross with its fake diamond.
This black and muddy claw at my neck.

*sunset blood sweat gossamer and wood ...*
*we should meet again in paradise ...*

The eyes stare back from the sea, blue domes.
Swollen copulas of soul.

*sunset blood sweat gossamer and wood ...*

I was only a man of driftwood who rose and fell to your tides,
            sculpted from you.
The fetched limb
*into your hands ...*

of your own resolve
to make me a shadow, a face
for the ivy fingers
learning to read the balconies
draped in green
and bougainvillea fire, learning to read this into existence
on a motel bed
where they were drawn by a light that shone *vacancy*.

Bones cast down point to the future
of some things that will never be.
They merely cross in the dark, twin, and
confuse the pronouns
until we cannot say each other's name
any more than we can say the name of God.

A man scratches and prepares to crow.

The world does not depend on you,
says the mirror.
Or your ten-penny book.

And the people you love are afraid of you.
You babble in the streets.
Strangers would rather not see you.
You hold out your wounded hands as they pass
but the coins you beg fall through their holes.

*　*　*

4:30 AM
A man is clawing at the dirt and preparing to crow.
I roll back the stone to uncover the stars.

# The Dream of the Cross

Remember the day you came back from the water,
which you tried to walk across
but failed
and now you're floating in the dream of world.

*Write about that,* you said.

You went looking for the words washed out to sea,
dissolved in salt.

You dove to set the anchor free
unconscious of the meters
going deeper into sleep, till, comatose,
breathing through a tube,
you saw not through tunnels into light
but a portal into death, the ship
reclining on its side. The eye
of God
        plucked out
and it looked on you as nothing.
Your body vanished.
No one claimed you.
You were a stranger.

*Write about that,* you said.
Ocean currents when the moon is full,
a shipwreck with its mast black cross.

Remember how cold the water was …
how deep you went,
how you ran out of air, a breathless form, a silence large
          and blue,
a fish in the eye of God
          that opens and closes his mouth, and still no words.
Your deafness—
that's His word
          like a feather
fallen from the moon,

your head so full of air it makes you dumb,
your lungs balloon with the language that will die with you,
your index finger unclips the belt. A thumb
presses the button that will end all time

                    and you ascend.

# Lost Gospels

It was in a village in the south, remember?
Quiet days in the yard of a ruined church.
Grass curving away from the stone fragments.
Processionals of ivy
and the *palomas* crooned in consolation the palimpsest
of now and then,
and signs went undivined in His "labyrinth of solitude"—
It's true.
There are no open doors.

It was from the village
my letters took weeks to reach you.

Here and there,
tanks, machine guns, the brown boys in their flak jackets
and Teflon helmets
posed in the corners of the square
or peered from the bell towers
like visitors to the nativity.

You stayed awhile with me
under the parasols of palms and Tule.
Leaves shuffled.
Colored lights shown through the crêpe paper flags,
and we danced to the *tamborazos* till you disappeared.

Then a fire rained
and for a thousand years
it finally dawned,

this hollowness.
Nights the rain came through the broken windows
and soaked the bed.
A poor rat scurried under my chair to dry off.

I wrote there the long letters on torn,
brown paper bags,
seeing the words flicker in candlelight—
each said *love ... love ...*

And once,
*"we have taken the town."*
Somewhere over the dark, green hills,
a river carried away the bodies of our friends.

It couldn't last.
We'd taken the message so far.
I couldn't say anymore what you looked like.
I couldn't remember my own face
after their bombs had shattered the mirrors.
I tried to turn the blood to wine, and the wine to words

to write to you just once more,
but in all this madness
I took to dancing drunken and alone
and I danced and danced under the trees so long
the wind and rain in their limbs became your voice.

# Lazarus, His Body Bag

Mary, my angel you wind you heavy sigh,
sleep in the shadow of your baby
in the room where you tuck me away,
where my eyes as priests—dark,
fall heavy on you
in the room where they've taken the blades
from the clock
and all the sharp edges.
A nurse through the black backside of a mirror looks in:
    —dirty boy,
little trash can baby-man—
and sees a chrysalis, guilty, hanging.

I lived like that in a body bag, a sweet goodnight suspended there.

In the first room, blue room,
they slapped me around and told me to breathe!
Pass through for the sake of the world, the needle.
Doctors
Nurses
Horsemen
Pass through my eye.
Come into the room that is filling with darkness, dark female
blood
and bloody altars.
The blue blue flames of beyond.
The vapor trail of beyond.

Take these pieces
stitched from old suits ripped apart

like the stories of the men who wore them—
a heavy gray wool like sleep, brown wool, dark blue—and
stitch them again into new.
Rocking and rocking
sew the new blue song with a long sticky hair.
Call them the petals of a rose and the Marquis de Sade,
tossing them, one by one
on a pile of dung.

Room number 2 was reserved
for the boy and girl,
its walls papered by a wasp
and writing on the walls to record rotations
of the sun and moon, the naked bed
made out of stone
to contain a madness
but sings out where she buried her child
because he was crying or whining like a locust at the dusk.

Room number 3—just basic.
Hospital white like a wedding gown.
Room you get shit into like the rich jewels
that flow from the wounds of Christ.
A sacrifice—
bright diamond she slips from her finger and deposits.
Elizabethan room for an Island Queen—
"Every woman must assassinate one man."

And the very last room?
That's where time hasn't any arms or edges
and no future, no dividing sweep
but a space to make of these stones a house, a room, a container,
poem to order its madness;
church to house its psychotic martyr;
hysterical woman to carry the child,

silence to pattern in cycles of thirteen years
that drills its way out of stone
and by the end of summer, leaves the delicate, glass body
attached to the trees I climbed and vanished in the leaves.

# The Betrayal

First she
removed her finger
and gave it to me.
Then her left eye.
Then her left ear
so I might touch, see, hear
a little bit of what she knew.

I wanted her to stop
and also I didn't want her to stop.
A leg from the thigh down.
Her arm.
Pretty soon there will be nothing left.

Then she pulled out her other eye
that contained a distant city in a fog.
It is a gift, a crystal ball to guide you, an ornament,
an oracle.

Then she gave me her ear, which was filled with voices.
Some pleasant. Others low and brutal.

Last, she gave me her vagina, the primordial nest
that fell from a tree in the wind.
It was torn and its stitches were crude.
I came so close to her soul
I could almost hold it in my hand.

She had given me herself, a rose, infinity
that lives inside of her. Petal after petal I took and took
to see her soul
and I didn't see it.
She was lost in the crowd.
With one hand left, she gave it to me to hold,
and I let it go in the crowd.

# The Avenue of Mysteries

Walk with me on the Avenue of Mysteries.
Walk with me in the widening circle of kindred spirits.
Through the torch light blue, dark blue darkening
the dormant fields to the end of each furrow,
through the storm's dark blue and shudder of sudden wind—
this is my body, to have and to hold,
white as a Weeping Cherry,
the white flag of surrender, white as a sheet so light
it is no burden at all to have and to hold.
Here, east of winter, where you have opened
this letter, I wake from a long sleep.
As you read, I turn into wind changing course toward home ...
with a poem on silence and time:
*An old man reaches a river, tired, and lies down.*
*Across the river, he sees the village*
*where he was born.*
It is a poem about dying
only when we have lived, and about
circles, or
the other way around.
It's not about the words.
We chase after the thing we want
and the person we love feels lost.

That is what I meant to say.
I give you this. My shell.
I don't need it anymore.

Walk with me in the aisles,
into the valley where there is no king,
no certainty,
no light
but a dark red peony.

# Blind Girl by the Louvre

What experience most desires is to be forgotten—
like pennies I toss in the Seine
or buttons come undone and lost.

She sees through me to a mirror, and further on, a meadow
which we say is night, a velvet glove of shadow,
the whisper nylons whisper when they shed.

She carries with her something of my past,
a night, wet and lovely
a river that feels its way to the horizon.

She is the veil, the white rose moon.
She feels—with wind where eyes once were—my looking

and my longing as I cannot capture her
in oils, naked to the sun, beside the willows on the Seine.

# Smoke Rising through the Trees

Smoke floats up
from the cook fires and into the trees
where we lived
   —darting from branch to branch as swallows—
the pure life, reaching and twisting toward the sky
reflecting its vast and empty nest
where we lived
and also where we could dig a fine and spacious grave
that would be large enough for such a life.

# A Christmas Letter to My Daughter

Dear Sophia,
You would be 16 this Christmas.
It's the time of year relatives send out boring letters
and brag about their kids.

I'm sorry, but I quit sending cards and rarely write letters.
When I do, I don't even mention you.

It's as if you were far away in a manger with no crib,
just that metal table for surgery
and late into the night the surgeon's light illuminated your wee
    twittering heart
while I paced in the waiting room waiting for an epiphany,
not realizing that you were the angel, the revelation and the
    star—fleeting.

Your first steps! Straight into the dark ...
So I was angry a long time.
"Suffer the little children ..." I heard, and other fairy tales.
I would have gladly read them to you, the nightmares we tell our
    kids:
Bible verses, witches that capture you in the woods, fatten you up
    and eat you;
ghouls to make you into soup, more Bible verses ...

What would you be like had you survived?
Would you still be calling me "Daddy"?
You would have a boyfriend with pimples:
I'd be threatening him with my eyes, asking if he'd like to see inside
    my gun safe.

You probably wouldn't even like me anymore ...
Mandatory Intro to Adolescence, Unit One: Defy thy father and
    refuse his name.

And how like your mother you'd be?
With her long black hair, which she straightened in vain to look
    more white.
Or would you have more love for who you are, dimples, drool, and all?

The truth is, you wouldn't like me if you knew me now.
Nobody likes the joyless old man who has no Christmas spirit—but
it's true, the nativity at the church on the corner
has no appeal for me.
It's a Hallmark setting for "families," and Christmas is for "families."
Their damn colored lights sucking power from the grid,
plastic shepherds staring clueless and dumb in the cold.
And Mary and Joseph clearly made the whole thing up.
"I already know where babies come from," you might have said,
had I ever gotten the chance to explain it.

And for some reason, a lot of people think this is the only time of
    year
when there are poor and homeless who might like to eat a decent
    meal.

So no, you probably wouldn't like me, little darling.

And things got so much worse ...
Your mother lost her mind when you left. Just lost herself ...
I don't know if her accident was even an accident,
but either way she went looking for you.
I'd like the think she found you, but I don't.

So whiskey kept me warm.
For a long time, it was me and my pal, Jack.
Women would come and go ...
(They see a man down and think they can fix him.)

That's when I said to myself, okay, what the fuck, and I went to the
     war—the war
that began when you died and the one that's still going on—and
     there
I saw a lot of kids die, but none of them were you.

Still waiting for some wise men to show up.
Been a lack of wisdom lately.
And Jesus might have wept—for all of us—but my bet is he's still
     weeping
especially for those of us who cannot.

# A Child Playing with Matches

There is a child playing with matches, playing
at kissing, a fire in fits and starts
by the end of August
when the sun is sinking like a ship on fire.

There is a young girl
and a kiss
by the end of August.

My heart sinks like an anchor through the deep
and a bird flies from its nest.
The woods are shaggy with leaves, and wet.

I'm sorry but that's all I can remember now.

There is a scarecrow in a field
ruing the way and directing my life.
Time wore his clothes right off.
Wind spun its gold back to straw.

# An Elegy

We danced in the square by the fountains,
your gold earrings catching the sun, catching
the eye of every man and woman.

You played with the wind in my hair.
You teased.
You cast wide invisible nets with your hands when you spoke.
You took my hand
and the world was jealous of me for being with you—

caught in a sudden rain,
under the eaves
but the waters rose and took us up and across in a boat
adrift,
    on fire,
a light
to find the path in the privacy of night, passage to a room where

behind us, doors back have closed
and with no thought at all, you lift me up,
dropping
my ragged clothes
to join—lover to lover
changing bodies.

The darkness is wet.
The wet roads bend in the darkness. The light
plays tricks.

I write this from my cell by a candle
when you are driving in the dark and rain.

# Sitting by a Warm Fire

Robert Bly,
    Talking to you is like sitting by a warm fire
with a cup of tea.
Certain teas give a man strange dreams.
The other night I sat beside a sleeping beauty …
all night, sat beside her, watching her sleep.
I thought, I want to put my finger in her open mouth.

I play both sides of a game of Chess
castling myself in opposing corners
like unwilling boxers.

Then there was dawn
and mist.

The sleeping beauty would not wake.
And the windows turned to old gray photographs.

# Swallows

*for Laura and Sophia*

*One day in October, the swallows were suddenly gone—and so was I.*


1


I step out of a valley carved by an old river
    and into the desert—which way? I ask
the prophet with a lazy eye. Which? where dry leaves drift,
    burning, erasing the places we passed, the signposts:

CHILDREN FORGET THEIR PARENTS

WOMAN WHOSE NAME I DON'T REMEMBER

THIS DOG BITES.

Her music was so sorrowful with beauty—
    the finger-tip veil of an idea, irreparable length of one's life
in the body of a terminal stranger, oneself, opalescent, shimmering
    and trailing the bride white gown of its coffin.

She lay under the pirúl with the wind entangled in its arms
    and smoke from sandalwood.
She suffered the sting of the flower.
Her body held onto its heat like a sea, and the sun went down
    like a ship on fire.

There is rest in change and rest in letting the lightning steer.
The dry bed of the river forks and veers away as if looking for you
    in a desert.
Some hold on to each other and won't let go even after breath is
    gone.


2


Shouldn't you be finished being dead?
Return to where knowing remembers before memory knows.
Ah, but you do. You know.
We are, you and I, one opalescent word—
drifting aloft, auroral and soft, a man and woman
whose compass whirled once around the world and stopped.

Lift me with the animal inside, rising and twisting
    in its shell.


3


Raspberries, cold
in the icy morning
shine in the gauzy mist ...
One, swollen, I gently loose, letting it wet my fingers, crimson ...
Leave the pale ones on the vine, letting the stalk fall back
in the weft of fern's wet smell and ether from the pines,
the magic in her nearness,
So delicate.
Perfect.
Raspberries,
      embers, red, darkening in my hand.

4

The world has left a note inside my sleeping.
But I am not ready to wake; I am not ready to leave this clarity
    behind.
Nor willing to come down from the cold mountain.

Perhaps I will come
when I have something to say that is as beautiful as
this wind that strums the pine it passes through.


5

The caress
of your fingers through hair ...
a blessing, as it was
at the beginning of the world
when there was yet no you, no paths to follow:
at each crossroad
each station and checkpoint where we pause
to consider our love.
Only the delicate dice of your fingers—


6

Clarity turns out to be an invisible form of sadness.

I journeyed to cities and continents, following swallows.

The lights of the boats illuminate
in lavenders and lilacs, the left and right banks, casting driftnets of
    shadows

from magnolias and mimosas across the gray façades, revealing
     smooth stone
                    and black lacy iron across bridges;
rapid streets and slower alleys converge and reach back
to the sound of chiming dishes, animated talk and sirens,
windows of silver ocean perch, blue mussels, lemons ...
Everywhere the smell of wine, perfumes, wet cobblestones.
Brass and white marble.

                    *   *   *


If the city seems clear, it may be because
the air is cool and motionless
while the Metro sends vibrations through the pavement.
Pedestrians bid for the streets with cars.
The bookstalls sell the best literature and the worst.
Straight buildings and even streets or even streets and cobbled
     alleys,
leaning each into each like friendly drinkers.
Time past and time present are swallows, curved and linear.
The arching note of a clarinet slurs just inside the mouth of the
     Metro.


7


Locusts whined in the dusk—then
left their delicate shells on the elms, and singing,
departed.
Holding one up to fading light,
I did not see how beautiful ... your song.

                    *   *   *

Then nothing remained but songs
like nothing remains like stones that suffered the same sun,
each day,
the same cold.

I had one to sing to my lover, to her naked, death-infested body,
one to her tear-smeared face in my lap.
And one to sing against a ceiling of beliefs—

*   *   *

The city in its crisis of color:
Magnolias bloom and the sun aligns with the windows of the
    cathedral.
Each flying buttress itself a stroke of time, keeping perfect shadows—
thunderhead blue vaulting the blond fields
and the shudder of thunder, receding.

Inside, the air is a cold remembrance, a smell like the soil of March,
or ether in grass after gusting rain

        letting go of the past, the mirrored arcades
with their columns of rain—

The past yet still present in her tangled sheets—as if

wandering in passages through her body, open doors
and empty rooms, subways, finding in her
caught in branches of rain
the webs of memory echoing in the subterranean,

traveling through her
wondering if I am dust

or if she is, dust and darkness,
its song of opalescence
showering down in the ether.

I fling myself
scatter myself on broken stones
beside her, joined like two stones joined
to make one arch,
one tributary moment, infinitely receding, opening, vanishing.

# Along the Avenues

Along the avenues
the travelers are months and years.

The ones who float past park benches
have taken their lives for granted.

For many years
people have perished along the avenues.

Others have taken off their shoes
to share a pot of tea.

I am surprised by a cloud
so complete in its wandering.

# Acknowledgements

*The Tenderness and the Wood* was made possible by two generous grants: the National Endowment for the Arts and the ConaCulta (Mexico's National Endowment).

Many of the poems first appeared in journals and anthologies: "Sappho's Child" and "Reading Palms in the Morgue" are in *Devouring the Green*, Jaded Ibis Press (but "Sappho's Child appears here as the condensed poem, "Lazarus, His Body Bag"). "Winter Signs" is in *The St. Petersburg Review*, "Zócalo As the Sun Goes Down" and "The Angel over Mexico City" appeared in *Colere* and were also translated and anthologized in *La región menos transparente*, Polytecnico University Press; "The Betrayal" won the New Hampshire Poetry Contest and appeared in *Sign Posts*; "Transfiguration" appeared in *The Café Review.* "Sources of Light" was published and received Honorable Mention in *Prairie Schooner*; "Lost Gospels" appeared in *The American Literary Review*; "Lines Written from the State Hospital" first appeared with the title "Omaha" in *El Financiero* newspaper in translation by Lillian van den Broeck; "Crows" appeared in *The Boston Review* and was subsequently translated by Ali Chumacero and published in Mexico; "Melissa's White Dress" appeared in *The Boston Phoenix*; "The Flood" appeared in *The New England Review*; "Anniversary" was published in *The Denver Quarterly*; "Puget Sound" was published under the title "To My Wife" by the *Antioch Review*; "The Sex Therapist" was published with several companion pieces in *Field*, but I chose to strike the poem. *Tupelo Quarterly* published "I Am Fly" and "Post Cards from Winter." Thomas Sayers Ellis chose "The Tenderness and the Wood" and "Swallows" for *Giantology*.

Thanks goes to Ilya Kaminsky for reordering the placement of one of the poems in a more sensible way. Also, thank you *American*

*Poetry Review* for publishing some of my Africa poems under the name of one of your assistant editors who shadowed Ruth Stone to my apartment in New York and took them. I'd also like to thank Galway Kinnell, Brenda Hillman, Ellen Bryant Voigt, Tom Lux, Robert Hass, and Robert Bly for their generous attention to earlier drafts of this book.

# About the Author

MARLON L. FICK holds a BA from the University of Kansas, an MA from New York University, and PhD from the University of Kansas. He is author of two poetry collections, a book of short stories, and the novel *The Nowhere Man* (Jaded Ibis, 2015), and is editor/translator of *The River Is Wide / El río es ancho: Twenty Mexican Poets* (New Mexico, 2005), as well as *XEIXA: 14 Catalan Poets* (Tupelo, 2018). Awarded fellowships from the U.S. National Endowment for the Arts, ConaCulta in Mexico, and Institut Ramon Llull in Catalonia, he now teaches at the University of Texas—Permian Basin.